Writing DoodleLoops

Creative Whole Language Activities for Beginning Writers

written and illustrated by
Sandy Baker

Copyright © 1994, Good Apple

ISBN No. 0-86653-790-2

Printing No. 98

Good Apple
A Division of Frank Schaffer Publications, Inc.
23740 Hawthorne Boulevard
Torrance, CA 90505-5927

A Word About *Writing DoodleLoops*

The DoodleLoops included in this book are a unique learning tool. They involve little or no teacher preparation and offer incredible results. The stimulating, thought-provoking illustrations naturally lead the children into the world of creative writing. Used as a daily writing activity, DoodleLoops offer enrichment for all ability levels. They afford you the opportunity to teach sentence structure, the elements of a story, the use of descriptive words, spelling, punctuation, and so much more. And above all, they stimulate creative thinking! What a sense of accomplishment you'll feel as you see your students' writing skills grow dramatically over the course of a year.

Directions for Use

The DoodleLoops program spans a number of grade levels and can be used with beginning as well as advanced writers. We have included Directions for Beginning Writers and Directions for Advanced Writers. Choose the directions that are appropriate for your students.

Directions for Beginning Writers

How to Begin

1. Use a demonstration Writing DoodleLoop (page 1) to introduce the Writing DoodleLoops concept.

2. Display the DoodleLoop in clear view of all of the students. Read the question "Who am I?" to the class. Then let the children brainstorm ideas in sentence form, such as "I am a monster." "I am an alien." "I am a scary space creature."

3. Choose one of the sentences, such as "I am a monster," and spend a substantial amount of time discussing how to "sound out" the words that the children don't already know how to spell. Emphasize that any spelling is acceptable. List the children's spelling suggestions on the board or on chart paper, such as:

> "I am a mnstr."
> "I am a mnr."
> "I m a mnsr."

4. Distribute the first Writing DoodleLoop to the children. Tell them to use their imaginations and to think of many possibilities before beginning to write. Encourage them to take their time, work carefully, and come up with their own unique ideas. At first, expect a short sentence or two from the majority of the children. However, if you have advanced writers in your class, encourage them to write more complex descriptions or stories. It is very important to encourage the children as they tackle the first DoodleLoop. It is helpful to circulate throughout the class as the children write, offering praise and assistance.

Daily Usage and Expectations

1. In order to develop and stimulate the children's ability to think and express themselves creatively, it is suggested that one DoodleLoop be given daily.

2. It is important to continually encourage the children to:

   • think of many possibilities for stories or descriptions before beginning to write

   • think of unique ideas

   • work neatly and carefully

   • leave appropriate spaces between their words

3. As the year progresses, encourage your students to write longer and more detailed stories. You may use DoodleLoops to teach the following:

   • proper capitalization and punctuation

   • use of descriptive words

   • how to write a complete story, including a beginning, middle, and end

   Each time you wish to introduce a new skill, use a DoodleLoop to model your expectations.

4. Optional: You may wish to write the correct spellings above the words the children write on their DoodleLoops. If you do so, emphasize that this is not a correction. The correct spelling is provided to help the children remember what they have written so that they may reread their work and share it with their families and classmates.

Published by Good Apple © 1994, Sandy Baker

GA1484

Directions for Advanced Writers

How to Begin

1. Use a demonstration Writing DoodleLoop (page 1) to introduce the DoodleLoop concept:

2. Display the DoodleLoop in clear view of all of the students. Read the question "Who am I?" to the class. Let the children brainstorm ideas, and list them on the chalkboard or on chart paper.

3. Choose one idea from the list. Discuss various ways to expand the idea into a story (with a beginning, middle, and end) or a descriptive narrative. Using chart paper, the chalkboard, or an overhead projector, model an example of each.

(Story)

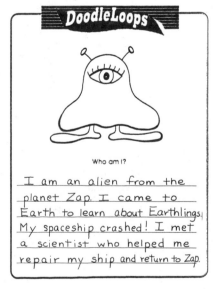

(Descriptive Narrative)

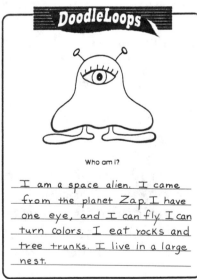

4. Distribute the first DoodleLoop to the children. Tell them to use their imaginations and to think of many possibilities before beginning to write. Encourage them to take their time, work carefully, and come up with their own unique ideas.

Published by Good Apple © 1994, Sandy Baker

GA1484

Daily Usage and Expectations

1. In order to develop and stimulate the children's abilities to think and express themselves creatively, it is suggested that one DoodleLoop be given daily.

2. As the year progresses, encourage your students to write longer and more detailed stories. For children who need additional paper, a master of lined paper is provided at the back of this book.

3. You may use the DoodleLoops to introduce more advanced skills, such as:

   • the use of proper punctuation and capitalization

   • the use of quotation marks

   • character development

   • paragraph formation

   • different types of writing, such as persuasive, narrative, poetry, etc.

   Each time you wish to introduce a new skill, use a DoodleLoop to model your expectations.

4. Conferencing: In order to help your children become more proficient writers, you may find it helpful to conference with them from time to time.

Published by Good Apple © 1994, Sandy Baker

GA1484

The Importance of Sharing

1. It is essential that the children have a vehicle for sharing their DoodleLoops in order to reinforce their ideas, to have support and feedback from their classmates, and to encourage divergent thinking.

2. The children may share their work in a variety of ways. You may choose one or more of the following:

   Daily Sharing: Share the DoodleLoops as a group. If time allows, each child may share his or her DoodleLoop with the class. If not, four or five children may share daily so that over the course of a week, all of the children have had one turn to share.

   Bulletin Boards: Display some of the more complex and creative DoodleLoops on a special bulletin board, or if space allows display all of the children's DoodleLoops.

   Overhead Transparencies: Each day you may wish to have one child make an overhead transparency of the DoodleLoop. After the other children in the group have completed their DoodleLoops, you can share the overhead with the class.

   Sharing with Another Class: You may wish to have your class or a group of your students share their DoodleLoops with another classroom.

   Class Library: You may wish to have the children make covers for some of their longer DoodleLoops. Put these DoodleLoops in a special place designated as your Class DoodleLoop Library.

Evaluation

1. Writing DoodleLoops give a good indication of the development of the children's writing skills, as well as their ability to express their thoughts and ideas clearly.

2. Writing DoodleLoops also give a good indication of the development of the children's phonetic skills.

3. If you wish to keep a record of the children's progress in the areas of writing and language arts, DoodleLoops are perfect for portfolio assessment.

Published by Good Apple © 1994. Sandy Baker

GA1484

Across the Curriculum Usage and Cooperative Learning

1. DoodleLoops may be used to reinforce skills being taught in other subject areas. They fit in beautifully with thematic units. You may use the DoodleLoops provided to tie in with:

> Holidays (Halloween, Thanksgiving, Valentine's Day, etc.)
> Affective Education (feelings and self esteem)
> Family Relationships
> Community
> Homes
> Transportation
> Geography
> Weather and Seasons
> Outer Space
> The Senses
> Plants
> Animals
> Insects

There is also a DoodleLoop on page 87 which has no illustration. You may use this DoodleLoop to insert any picture you wish that relates to any special subject matter that you may be teaching.

*Optional: You may also allow the children to create their own Doodle-Loops using the blank DoodleLoop.

2. The DoodleLoops may also be used as a cooperative learning tool. You may ask two or three children to work on a DoodleLoop together.

Family Involvement

1. At the beginning of the year it is helpful to write a letter to each child's family explaining the purpose of the DoodleLoops. A sample letter is provided on page viii.

2. It is very important that the children share their DoodleLoops with their families. They provide a wonderful connection between school and home, and families truly enjoy sharing with their children and watching their progress over the course of the year.

Enjoy the DoodleLoops!

They offer endless possibilities for learning
and for expanding creative awareness!

Acknowledgment

My deepest thanks to Donna Napolitano, devoted professional, for her encouragement and continual support.

Published by Good Apple © 1994. Sandy Baker GA1484

Dear Family,

This year your child will be working on some very special pages called Writing DoodleLoops. These DoodleLoops will be used as a tool to stimulate creative writing. The children will begin to write sentences and short stories about pictures that they see on a DoodleLoop page.

They will be spelling the words phonetically as they hear them. I encourage them to spell the words on their own, as correct spelling on DoodleLoops is not necessary. I may be writing the correct spelling above the children's words, but this is not to be viewed as a correction. I do this in order for the children to be able to reread their stories to their classmates and to you. If the correct spellings are not indicated, the children sometimes forget what some of the more difficult words are.

Please encourage your child to read his or her DoodleLoops to you. You will begin to see a natural improvement in the spelling as the year progresses. The children's stories will also become more involved and detailed over time.

DoodleLoops stimulate creative thinking and are excellent tools for teaching and reinforcing reading, phonics, spelling, and writing skills. Your involvement is a wonderful means of reinforcing your child's creativity and sparking the learning process.

Thank you so much for your cooperation, involvement, and support.

Sincerely,

Published by Good Apple © 1994, Sandy Baker

GA1484

Who am I?

_____

_____

_____

_____

_____

1

GA1484

Why am I so happy?

_____

_____

_____

_____

_____

DoodleLoops

Why am I crying?

_____

_____

_____

_____

_____

_____

_____

Published by Good Apple © 1994, Sandy Baker

GA1484

What do I see?

_____

_____

_____

_____

_____

DoodleLoops

What do I smell?

_____

_____

_____

_____

_____

_____

Published by Good Apple © 1994, Sandy Baker

GA1484

DoodleLoops

What do I hear?

_____

_____

_____

_____

_____

Published by Good Apple © 1994, Sandy Baker

GA1484

What am I dreaming about?

_____

_____

_____

_____

_____

_____

Published by Good Apple © 1994, Sandy Baker GA1484

Who am I?

_____

_____

_____

_____

_____

Who am I?

_____

_____

_____

_____

_____

_____

GA1484

Who am I?

_____

_____

_____

_____

_____

_____

GA1484

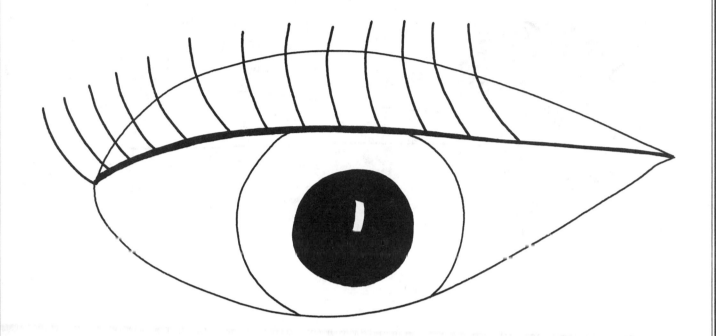

DoodleLoops

What am I?

_____

_____

_____

_____

_____

_____

Published by Good Apple © 1994, Sandy Baker GA1484

DoodleLoops

Who am I?

_____

_____

_____

_____

_____

Published by Good Apple © 1994. Sandy Baker

GA1484

DoodleLoops

Who am I?

GA1484

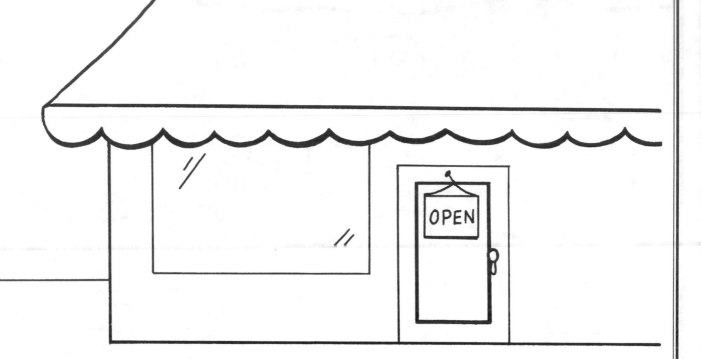

What is inside?

_____

_____

_____

_____

_____

_____

14

DoodleLoops

KEEP OUT!

What is behind this door?

_____

_____

_____

_____

_____

_____

Published by Good Apple © 1994. Sandy Baker

GA1484

DoodleLoops

Who are we?

_____

_____

_____

_____

_____

Published by Good Apple © 1994, Sandy Baker

GA1484

Who am I?

_____

_____

_____

_____

_____

GA1484

DoodleLoops

What is in the pot?

_____

_____

_____

_____

_____

_____

Published by Good Apple © 1994. Sandy Baker

GA148-4

DoodleLoops

What is in my hat?

_____

_____

_____

_____

_____

Published by Good Apple © 1994, Sandy Baker

GA1484

DoodleLoops

Who are we?

_____

_____

_____

_____

_____

GA1484

DoodleLoops

Who am I?

_____

_____

_____

_____

_____

_____

GA1484

DoodleLoops

Who am I?

_____

_____

_____

_____

_____

GA1484

Where am I going?

_____

_____

_____

_____

_____

GA1484

DoodleLoops

Who am I?

GA1484

DoodleLoops

What am I cooking?

_____

_____

_____

_____

_____

_____

DoodleLoops

Who am I?

_____

_____

_____

_____

_____

Who am I?

_____

_____

_____

_____

_____

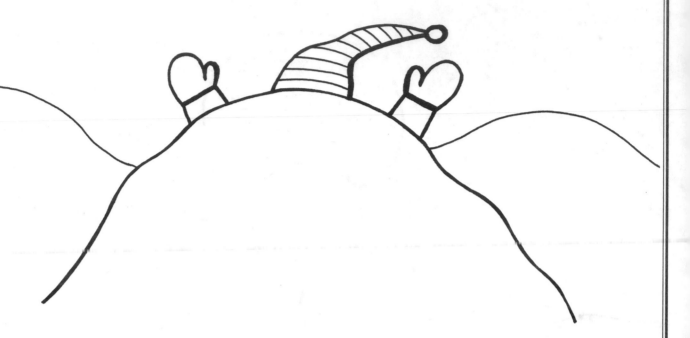

Who am I?

_____

_____

_____

_____

_____

_____

GA1484

GA1484

What am I thinking about?

_____

_____

_____

_____

DoodleLoops

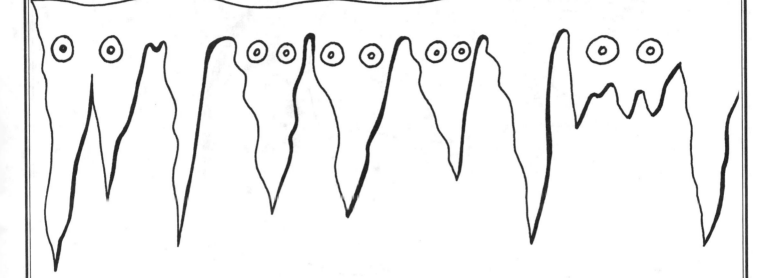

Who are we?

_____

_____

_____

_____

_____

_____

Published by Good Apple © 1994, Sandy Baker GA1484

DoodleLoops

Who am I?

_____

_____

_____

_____

_____

_____

Published by Good Apple © 1994, Sandy Baker

GA1484

DoodleLoops

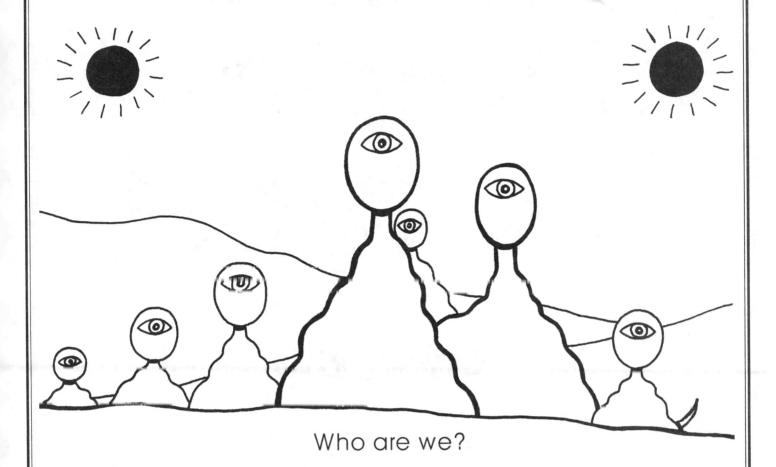

Who are we?

_____

_____

_____

_____

_____

_____

GA1484

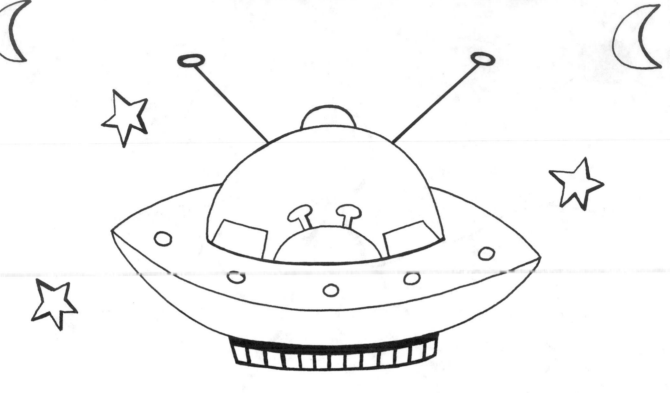

DoodleLoops

What am I?

_____

_____

_____

_____

_____

_____

_____

38

GA1484

Who are we?

_____

_____

_____

_____

_____

_____

Where are we?

_____

_____

_____

_____

_____

_____

_____

DoodleLoops

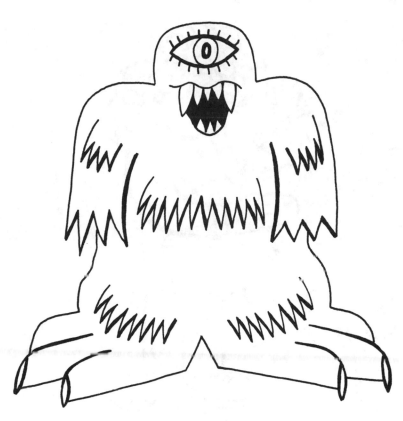

Who am I?

_____

_____

_____

_____

_____

_____

Published by Good Apple © 1994, Sandy Baker

GA1484

Who are we?

DoodleLoops

What am I?

_____

_____

_____

_____

_____

GA1484

DoodleLoops

Who am I?

_____

_____

_____

_____

_____

_____

Published by Good Apple © 1994, Sandy Baker GA1484

What am I?

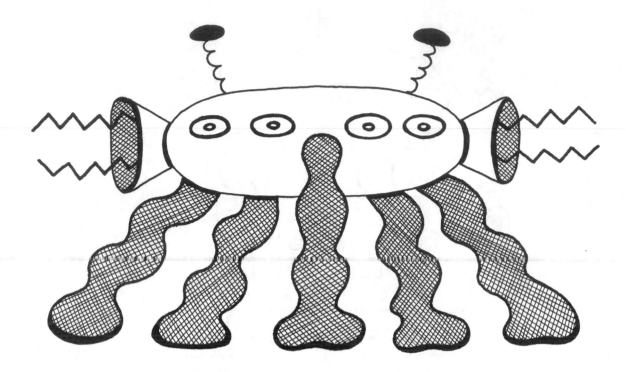

Who am I?

_____

_____

_____

_____

_____

_____

DoodleLoops

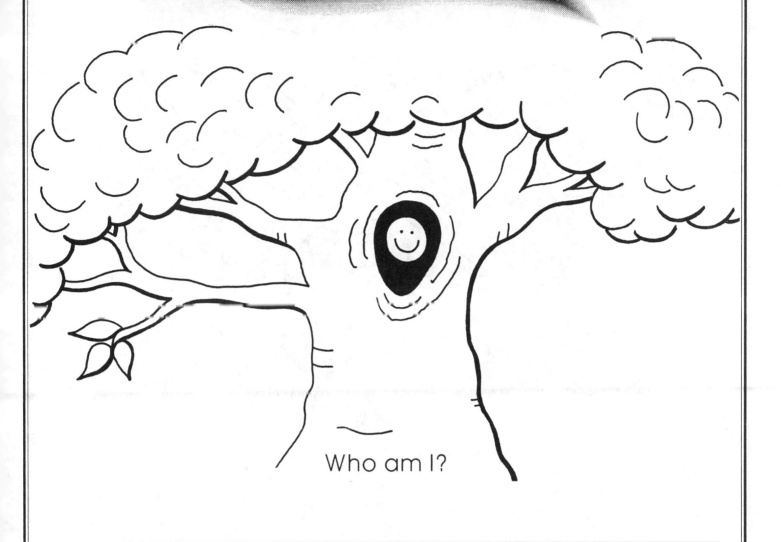

Who am I?

GA1484

Where am I?

Published by Good Apple © 1994, Sandy Baker

GA1484

Where am I?

_____

_____

_____

_____

_____

_____

Where am I?

_____

_____

_____

_____

_____

Published by Good Apple © 1994, Sandy Baker GA1484

DoodleLoops

Where am I?

_____

_____

_____

_____

_____

GA1484

Where am I?

Published by Good Apple © 1994, Sandy Baker

GA1484

DoodleLoops

What is happening?

_____

_____

_____

_____

_____

Published by Good Apple © 1994, Sandy Baker

GA1484

What is happening?

_____

_____

_____

_____

_____

Published by Good Apple © 1994, Sandy Baker

GA1484

DoodleLoops

What is happening?

_____

_____

_____

_____

_____

GA1484

DoodleLoops

Who am I?

_____

_____

_____

_____

_____

Published by Good Apple © 1994, Sandy Baker

DoodleLoops

Where are we going?

_____

_____

_____

_____

_____

_____

Published by Good Apple © 1994, Sandy Baker

GA1484

What am I?

_____

_____

_____

_____

_____

_____

_____

GA148

DoodleLoops

Where am I going?

_____

_____

_____

_____

_____

_____

Published by Good Apple © 1994, Sandy Baker

GA1484

DoodleLoops

Where am I going?

_____

_____

_____

_____

_____

_____

Published by Good Apple © 1994. Sandy Baker

GA148

DoodleLoops

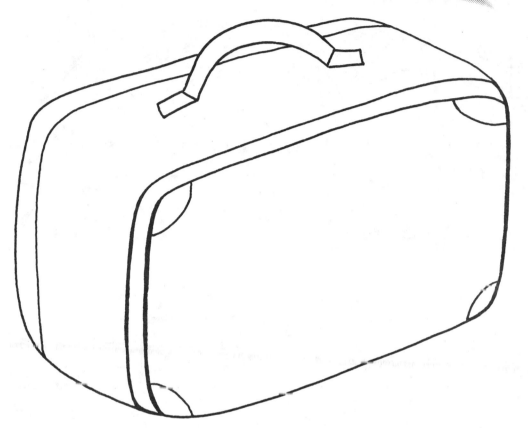

What is inside of me?

_____

_____

_____

_____

_____

_____

Published by Good Apple © 1994, Sandy Baker

GA1484

DoodleLoops

Who lives here?

_____

_____

_____

_____

_____

Published by Good Apple © 1994, Sandy Baker

GA1484

DoodleLoops

Who lives here?

_____

_____

_____

_____

_____

Published by Good Apple © 1994, Sandy Baker
GA1484

DoodleLoops

What is this?

_____

_____

_____

_____

_____

DoodleLoops

Who am I?

_____

_____

_____

_____

_____

_____

Published by Good Apple © 1994, Sandy Baker

GA1484

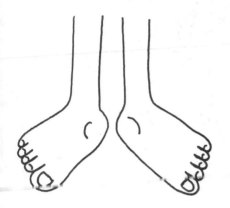 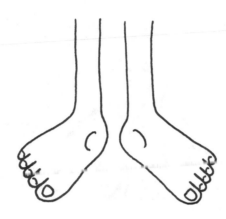 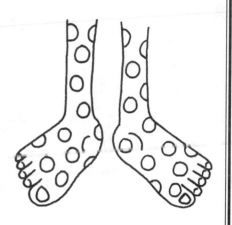

What are we?

_____

_____

_____

_____

_____

GA1484

What is happening?

_____

_____

_____

_____

_____

_____

_____

Published by Good Apple © 1994, Sandy Baker

GA1484

Who are we?

_____

_____

_____

_____

_____

GA1484

Who am I?

_____

_____

_____

_____

_____

_____

DoodleLoops

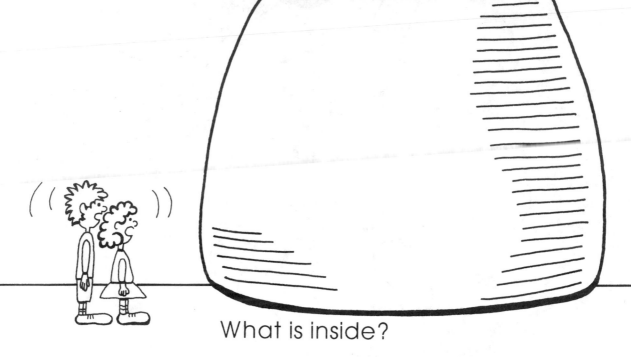

What is inside?

_____

_____

_____

_____

_____

Published by Good Apple © 1994. Sandy Baker

GA1484

What am I?

Published by Good Apple © 1994, Sandy Baker

GA1484

Who am I?

_____

_____

_____

_____

_____

Published by Good Apple © 1994, Sandy Baker

GA1484

What am I reading about?

GA1484

DoodleLoops

What is in here?

_____

_____

_____

_____

_____

Published by Good Apple © 1994. Sandy Baker

GA1484

DoodleLoops

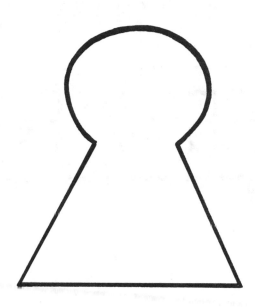

I am a keyhole.
What do you see through me?

GA1484

⬅ BEWARE!!!

What is this pointing to?

_____

_____

_____

_____

_____

Published by Good Apple © 1994. Sandy Baker

Who am I?

_____

_____

_____

_____

_____

Published by Good Apple © 1994, Sandy Baker

DoodleLoops

Who am I?

_____

_____

_____

_____

_____

GA1484

What do I see?

_____

_____

_____

_____

_____

_____

GA1484

What do we see?

_____

_____

_____

_____

_____

_____

DoodleLoops

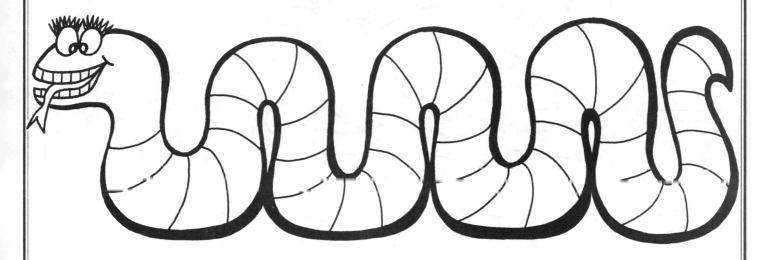

Who am I?

_____

_____

_____

_____

_____

GA1484

Who am I?

_____

_____

_____

_____

_____

GA148

DoodleLoops

Who are we?

_____

_____

_____

_____

_____

Published by Good Apple © 1994. Sandy Baker

GA1484

DoodleLoops

Who are we?

_____

_____

_____

_____

_____

Published by Good Apple © 1994. Sandy Baker

GA1484

What am I doing?

_____

_____

_____

_____

_____

_____

Published by Good Apple © 1994. Sandy Baker

GA1484

DoodleLoops

What do I see?

_____

_____

_____

_____

_____

GA148

GA1484